LIGHTNING BOLT BOOKS

Cool Kids Changing the World

Laura Hamilton Waxman

Lerner Publications • Minneapolis

For Miriam, who makes the world a better place by being in it —L.H.W.

Lerner Publications Company
An imprint of Lerner Publishing Group, Inc.
241 First Avenue North
Minneapolis, MN 55401 USA

For reading levels and more information, look up this title at www.lernerbooks.com.

Library of Congress Cataloging-in-Publication Data

Names: Waxman, Laura Hamilton, author.
Title: Cool kids changing the world / Laura Hamilton Waxman.
Description: Minneapolis : Lerner Publications, [2020] | Series: Lightning bolt books. Kids in charge! | Includes bibliographical references and index.
Identifiers: LCCN 2019017246 (print) | LCCN 2019019216 (ebook) | ISBN 9781541583245 (eb pdf) | ISBN 9781541577015 (lb : alk. paper) | ISBN 9781541589155 (pb : alk. paper)
Subjects: LCSH: Children—Political activity—Juvenile literature. | Social action—Juvenile literature.
Classification: LCC HQ784.P5 (ebook) | LCC HQ784.P5 W39 2020 (print) | DDC 320.083—dc23

LC record available at https://lccn.loc.gov/2019017246

Manufactured in the United States of America
1-46723-47714-7/9/2019

Table of Contents

Big Hearts, Big Ideas

The world is full of problems to solve. Luckily, creative kids are ready to help.

These kids have big hearts and big ideas too. They want to make the world a better place, and they're finding cool ways to do it.

Speaking Out

Some kids notice unfairness in the world. They raise their voices when something is unfair.

Malala Yousafzai

Malala was eleven when new leaders took over her town in Pakistan. They stopped girls from going to school. She said girls have the right to an education. The leaders tried to silence her, but she kept speaking out.

Kids Helping Kids

Kids solve problems all around the world. One way is by helping other kids.

Buddy benches help kids make friends.

Samantha Vance

Samantha Vance collected bottle caps to create buddy benches. Kids sit on the benches when they need a friend, and other kids invite them to play.

Marley Dias

Marley Dias loves to read. But she had a hard time finding books about black girls like her.

Marley asked people to help her collect one thousand books about black girls. She collected more than twelve thousand! She gave the books to schools and libraries. That way, lots of kids can read them.

Solving Problems

What do you do when you see someone who needs help? Some kids get to work.

Jahkil Jackson

Jahkil Jackson has given away thousands of "blessing bags" to help homeless people. His bags have helped people in the United States, Guatemala, Puerto Rico, and Eswatini.

Inside the bags are a water bottle, first aid kit, socks, and more.

FIRST AID

Sophie Cruz

Sophie Cruz was born in the United States. But her parents are from Mexico. They are immigrants seeking a better life.

Sophie speaks up for immigrants.

Some people treat immigrants unfairly. Sophie wants to change that. She gives powerful speeches about her parents and other immigrants.

Saving the Planet

Some kids want to protect our planet. They work hard to keep the planet healthy for all living things.

Ryan Hickman

Ryan Hickman started his own recycling company when he was three years old. His company collects bottles, cans, and other trash to recycle. He recycles to keep pollution far from the ocean.

Ryan picks up recycling in a car made just for kids.

Joris Hutchison

Joris Hutchison works to protect cheetahs. These animals are in danger of going extinct. Joris has raised thousands of dollars to protect cheetahs in Namibia. He gets the money from projects such as lemonade stands and garage sales.

Joris's hard work keeps cheetahs safe.

Kids are taking on big problems, helping one another, and protecting Earth. They're following their hearts and working hard to make a difference.

You Can Do It!

Do you want to change the world? Start by doing something helpful each day. Be kind to a classmate who is sad. Help your family recycle more. Save money for a cause you care about. Then get your friends, family, and neighbors involved. Start a project you can work on together.

Did You Know?

- Malala Yousafzai is the youngest person to receive the Nobel Peace Prize.

- Marley Dias wrote a book encouraging kids to keep changing the world.

- Jahkil Jackson's "blessing bags" have helped more than twenty thousand people.

Glossary

education: the learning of math, reading, and other things in school

extinct: no longer living

homeless: without a home of one's own

immigrant: a person who comes to live in a country from another country

pollution: something that makes the land, air, or water dirty and unsafe

recycling: using old plastic, metal, and paper to make something new

Further Reading

Be a Volunteer
https://kidshealth.org/en/kids/volunteering.html

Bullard, Lisa. *Go Green by Recycling.* Minneapolis: Lerner Publications, 2019.

Higginson, Sheila Sweeny. *Kids Who Are Changing the World!* New York: Simon Spotlight, 2018.

Kids for Cheetahs
http://www.kids4cheetahs.com

Project I Am
https://officialprojectiam.com

Ryan's Recycling
http://ryansrecycling.com

Yousafzai, Malala. *Malala: My Story of Standing Up for Girls' Rights.* New York: Little, Brown, 2018.

Index

Photo Acknowledgments

Image credits: Pixel-Shot/Shutterstock.com, p. 2; iStock/Getty Images, p. 4; Dmytro Zinkevych/Shutterstock.com, p. 5; Maskot/Getty Images, p. 6; Paul Pickard/Alamy Stock Photo, p. 7; Pahis/Getty Images, p. 8; The Daily Dispatch/Photographer, p. 9; Mike Windle/ Getty Images, p. 10; Utamaru Kido/Getty Images, p. 11; vgajic/Getty Images, p. 12; Magdalena photographer/Shutterstock.com, p. 13; ruangrit junkong/Shutterstock.com, p. 13; Victor Moussa/Shutterstock.com, p. 13; Vivien Killilea/Stringer/Getty Images, pp. 14, 15; Alex Bramwell/Getty Images, p. 16; MediaNews Group/Orange County Register/Getty Images, p. 17; ben landy/Shutterstock.com, p. 18; GNT STUDIO/Shutterstock.com, p. 19; wavebreakmedia/Shutterstock.com, p. 20; Thannaree Deepul/Shutterstock.com, p. 22.

Cover Image: MediaNews Group/Getty Images.

Main body text set in Billy Infant regular. Typeface provided by SparkType.